THE DOMINIE W
Migration

GRAHAM MEADOWS & CLAIRE VIAL

Contents

What Is Migration?	2
On the Wing	4
Long-Distance Fliers	6
Preparing for Migration	8
Knowing When to Leave	10
Finding Their Way	12
Traveling Together or Alone	14
Day Fliers and Night Fliers	16
Migration Routes	18
Dangerous Courses	20
Learning about Migration	22
Glossary	24
Index	24

DOMINIE PRESS
Pearson Learning Group

Brent geese migrating

An eastern towhee

What Is Migration?

Many birds do not live in the same place all year. They fly away to spend part of the year in a different place, and then they fly back again. This **cyclical** movement is called **migration**.

Birds migrate for one or more reasons to find
- A better food supply.
- A warmer place to spend winter.
- The best place to nest and raise their young.

Some birds, such as the eastern towhee, migrate a distance of only a few hundred miles.

Others, such as bar-tailed godwits, migrate more than 6,000 miles. They nest in western Alaska in the northern summer, and spend the southern summer in New Zealand.

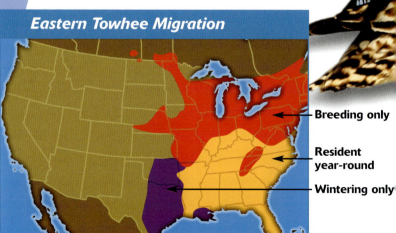

Eastern Towhee Migration

- Breeding only
- Resident year-round
- Wintering only

Bar-tailed godwits and red knots resting

Bar-tailed Godwit Migration

Godwit Northward Route

Godwit Southward Route

A bar-tailed godwit

More than one-third of all bird **species** migrate.

3

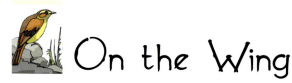
On the Wing

As autumn approaches, many birds in Europe and North America migrate south to spend the winter in warmer areas. In spring, they fly back again.

Grey phalaropes breed in the high **Arctic** and then fly south to winter at sea off the coast of western Africa.

Barnacle geese, which breed on islands northwest of Norway during the summer, spend the winter along the coasts of Ireland, England, northern France, Belgium, Holland, West Germany, and Denmark.

Some birds migrate from high places to low places, and back again. For example, snow partridges in the **Himalayas** spend the summer months high up in the mountains. In winter, they migrate down to the warmer valleys.

A grey phalarope

Great egrets migrate short distances.

Barnacle Goose Migration

Barnacle geese

In Australasia, few birds migrate the very long distances that many European and North American species do.

5

Long-Distance Fliers

American golden plovers have one of the longest migrations of any North American bird. They nest in Alaska and northern Canada during the northern summer. As winter approaches, they fly south to spend the southern summer in South America, a journey of more than 2,500 miles. In spring, they return northward again.

Arctic terns migrate farther than any other bird. They nest in the Arctic during the northern summer. They then fly about 11,000 miles to spend the southern summer in **Antarctica**. They return to the Arctic a few months later. Arctic terns feed on fish as they migrate.

An American golden plover

Each spring, red-eyed vireos migrate from their South American wintering grounds to breeding grounds in the eastern United States and Canada.

An Arctic tern on a nest

American Golden Plover Migration

Breeding only

Wintering only

Arctic Tern Southern Migration

Preparing for Migration

Birds have a special "body clock" that prepares them for migration. As winter approaches and days become shorter, their body clock changes the level of special chemicals, called **hormones**. These hormones tell the birds to get ready for the next migration.

Before a bird migrates, it must finish **molting** so that its feathers are in top condition for the long journey ahead. It must also eat extra food, which is stored under the skin as fat. The fat is used to provide the extra energy needed during migration.

A dunlin

A redshank

A Canada goose

Most birds gain about one-third of their body weight before a migration.

House martin in flight

Knowing When to Leave

As the time to migrate approaches, some birds become more restless. They start to fly around in **flocks**. The exact day of their departure may depend on the weather.

During migration, many birds frequently stop off at places along the way to feed and rest.

Some birds, such as house martins and swallows, do not need to stop off to feed. They simply catch flying insects while they are in the air.

Hermit thrushes breed in the northern United States and Canada, and fly south for the winter.

Wrybills shortly before migration

Long-billed dowitchers resting

A pigeon in flight

 # Finding Their Way

Birds use different methods to find their way, or to **navigate**. Some use landmarks, such as mountains, rivers, valleys, and coastlines. Some species use the sun to help them navigate. One example is the semi-palmated sandpiper, which breeds in the Arctic during summer and spends the winter months in South America.

Some birds, such as pigeons, also use their sense of smell to find their way.

Zebra finches only migrate during periods of extreme weather conditions, such as drought.

A semi-palmated sandpiper on the tundra

Some species of birds, such as willow warblers, fly by night, finding their way by using the stars.

Traveling Together or Alone

Ducks flying in a V-shape

A shining bronze-cuckoo eating a beetle larva.

Many birds migrate together in large groups, called flocks. Traveling together is safer, because it makes it more difficult for **predators** to pick out and attack a single bird.

Some birds, such as geese and pelicans, fly in a V-shape. This allows each bird to fly in the **slipstream**, or area of reduced air pressure, of the bird in front of it. A bird uses less energy while in a slipstream. Racing cyclists often use a similar formation.

Some birds, such as cuckoos, migrate alone.

Most migrating birds fly at heights of less than 5,000 feet. Some, such as waterfowl and shorebirds, fly higher. Bar-headed geese have been seen migrating at about 30,000 feet, higher than the Himalayan Mountains.

Curlews in flight

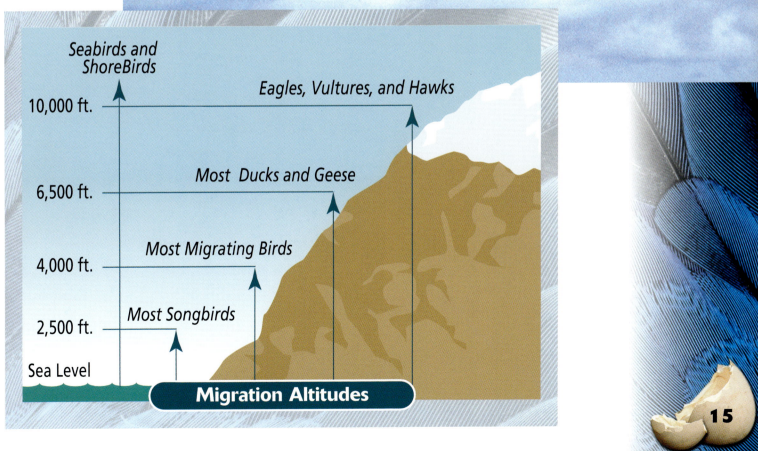

Migration Altitudes

- Seabirds and ShoreBirds — 10,000 ft.
- Eagles, Vultures, and Hawks — 10,000 ft.
- Most Ducks and Geese — 6,500 ft.
- Most Migrating Birds — 4,000 ft.
- Most Songbirds — 2,500 ft.
- Sea Level

The hermit thrush migrates at night.

Day Fliers and Night Fliers

Many large birds, such as sandhill cranes, tend to migrate during the day, landing from time to time to feed and rest. At night, the cranes roost in **wetlands**, where they are protected from most predators by a water barrier.

Swifts and swallows also migrate by day, but they feed while they are flying.

Many smaller birds tend to migrate during the night to avoid daytime predators. They rest and feed during the day.

Some birds, such as waterfowl, migrate both by day and by night.

Sandhill cranes in flight

A welcome swallow in flight

An Australasion gannet resting

Migration Routes

Most migrating birds follow specific routes, which are called **flyways**. Three of the largest flyways are between North America and South America, Europe and Africa, and East Asia and **Australasia**. Many land birds don't like to migrate over the sea, so these flyways allow them to fly over land as much as possible. They use the shortest routes possible when crossing over the sea.

Migrating seabirds do not need to fly over land as much as land birds. They can rest and feed on the sea.

Australasion gannets

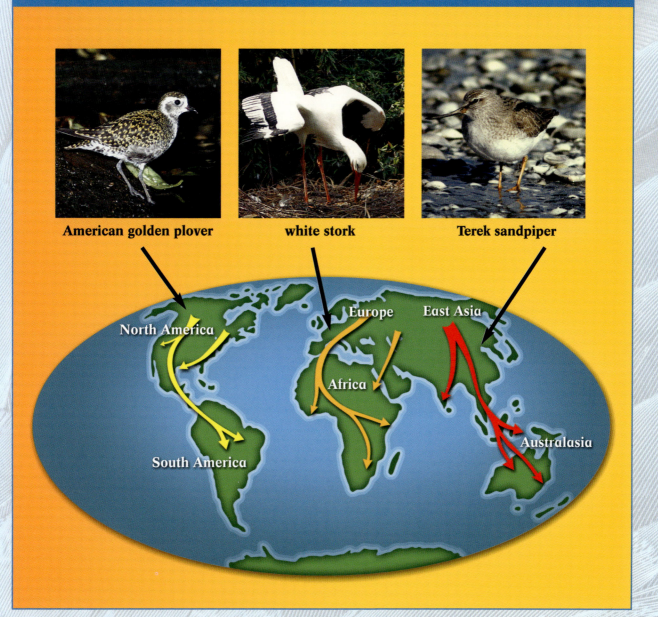

The Three Major Flyways and Examples of the Birds That Use Them

American golden plover — white stork — Terek sandpiper

A kitten with a dead bird

A dead gannet on a beach

 # Dangerous Courses

Migration is dangerous. In some cases, fewer than half of the birds that migrate in the fall survive to return the following spring.

Migration over water is one of the most dangerous times for small birds. Millions of them die at sea. These are often young birds, or birds that are blown offshore or forced down by bad weather.

There are other dangers too:
- Predators, such as birds of **prey** and household cats, attack migrating birds.
- Tall buildings, lighthouses, power lines, radio and television towers, and windows interfere with birds in migration.
- Destruction of natural **habitats** by humans poses a risk to birds' **survival**.
- Strong winds, storms, and bad weather can disrupt a migration.

Logging operations often destroy natural habitats where birds live.

Reflections in glass can confuse birds.

Large buildings create obstacles for migrating birds.

A girl using binoculars

 # Learning about Migration

Scientists use various methods to study bird migrations. The methods include bird-watching, viewing radar, radio tracking, and bird banding.

Bird-Watching
During migrations, many people use binoculars to watch and record bird movements.

Viewing Radar
Large flocks of birds show up on radar screens.

Radio Tracking
In radio tracking, scientists catch a bird and insert a **radio transmitter** under its skin. They then use a **radio receiver** to record the bird's position and follow its flight path.

Bird Banding
When bird banding, scientists catch a bird and place a metal or colored plastic ring on one of its legs. Each ring has a unique code made up of letters or numbers. If the bird is caught again, or if it is found dead, scientists can identify where it came from.

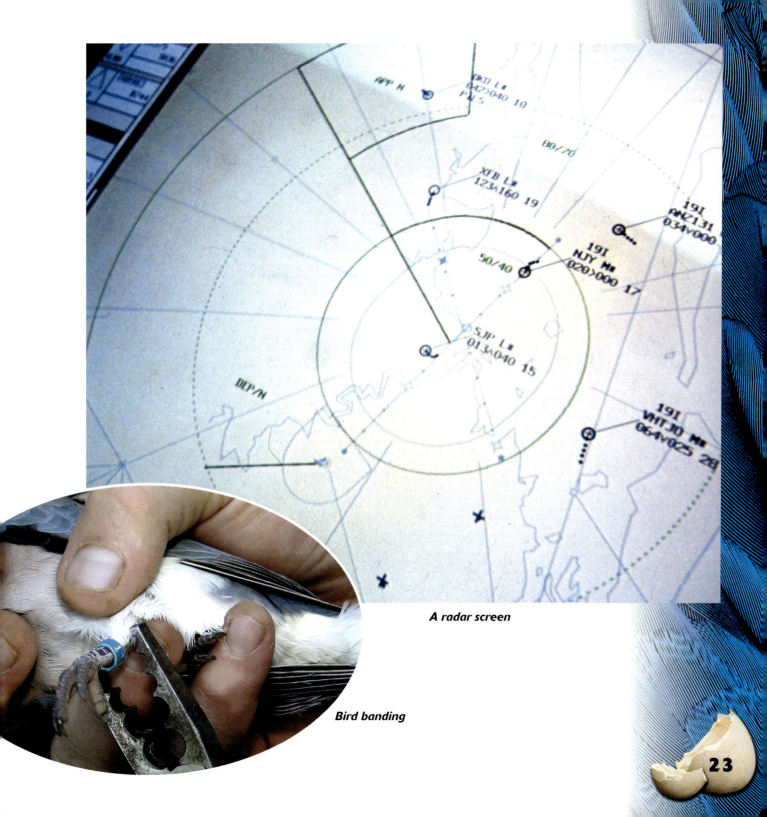

A radar screen

Bird banding

23

Glossary

Antarctica: A largely uninhabited continent surrounding the South Pole

Arctic: The cold, barren region surrounding the North Pole

Australasia: A region southeast of Asia and south of the equator made up of Australia, Tasmania, New Zealand, and Melanesia

cyclical: Repeated on a regular basis, as in the changing, recurring seasons

flocks: Groups of birds of the same kind that live together

flyways: Migration routes

habitats: The places where animals and plants live and grow

Himalayas: A 1,500-mile system of mountain ranges in Asia

hormones: Chemicals in the body that produce specific physical reactions

migration: The movement of one or more animals from one region or habitat to another in response to cyclical seasonal changes

molting: Shedding feathers, hair, or skin and replacing what is lost with new growth

navigate: To steer a course

predators: Animals that hunt, catch, and eat other animals

radio receiver: A mechanical device that detects and pinpoints signals sent by a radio transmitter

radio transmitter: A mechanical device that sends electronic signals

slipstream: An area of reduced air pressure and forward suction immediately behind a fast-moving animal or object

species: A group of animals or plants that have many physical characteristics in common

survival: Continued existence

wetlands: Marshes, swamps, or other areas of land where the soil near the surface is saturated or covered with water, often forming an ideal habitat for a variety of wildlife

Index

American golden plovers, 6
Antarctica, 6
Arctic, 4, 6, 12
Arctic terns, 6, 7
Australasia, 5, 18

bar-headed geese, 14
barnacle geese, 4, 5
bar-tailed godwits, 2, 3

bird banding, 22, 23
bird-watching, 22

cuckoos, 14

eastern towhee, 2

feathers, 8
flocks, 10, 14, 22
flyways, 18, 19

geese, 14
grey phalarope, 4

Himalayas, 4
hormones, 8
house martins, 10

pelicans, 14
pigeons, 12
predators, 14, 16, 20

radar, 22
radar screens, 22, 23
radio receiver, 22

radio tracking, 22
radio transmitter, 22

sandhill cranes, 16, 17
semi-palmated sandpiper, 12, 13
shorebirds, 14, 15
slipstream, 14
snow partridges, 4
swallows, 10, 16
swifts, 16

waterfowl, 14, 16
wetlands, 16
willow warblers, 13